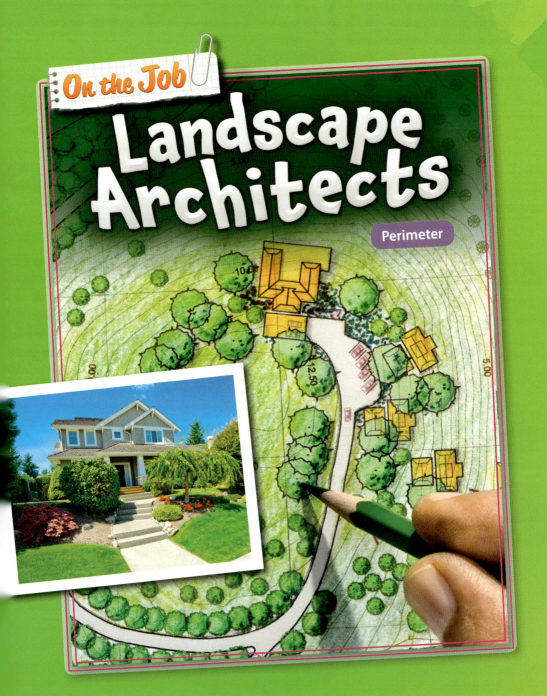

On the Job
Landscape Architects

Perimeter

Wendy Conklin, M.A.

Consultants

Michele Ogden, Ed.D
Principal, Irvine Unified School District

Jennifer Robertson, M.A.Ed.
Teacher, Huntington Beach City School District

Publishing Credits

Rachelle Cracchiolo, M.S.Ed., *Publisher*
Conni Medina, M.A.Ed., *Managing Editor*
Dona Herweck Rice, *Series Developer*
Emily R. Smith, M.A.Ed., *Series Developer*
Diana Kenney, M.A.Ed., NBCT, *Content Director*
Stacy Monsman, M.A., *Editor*
Kevin Panter, *Graphic Designer*

Image Credits: p. 15 James Davies/Alamy Stock Photo; all other images from Shutterstock and/or iStockphoto

Library of Congress Cataloging-in-Publication Data

Names: Conklin, Wendy.
Title: Landscape architects / Wendy Conklin, M.A.
Description: Huntington Beach, CA : Teacher Created Materials, 2017. | Series: On the job | Audience: K to grade 3. | Includes index.
Identifiers: LCCN 2016053561 (print) | LCCN 2017001954 (ebook) | ISBN 9781480758094 (pbk.) | ISBN 9781480758735 (eBook)
Subjects: LCSH: Landscape architects--Juvenile literature. | Landscape architecture--Juvenile literature.
Classification: LCC SB469.37 .C66 2017 (print) | LCC SB469.37 (ebook) | DDC 712--dc23
LC record available at https://lccn.loc.gov/2016053561

Teacher Created Materials

5301 Oceanus Drive
Huntington Beach, CA 92649-1030
http://www.tcmpub.com

ISBN 978-1-4807-5809-4
© 2018 Teacher Created Materials, Inc.
Made in China
Nordica.022017.CA21700227

Table of Contents

Landscape Architects 4

Getting Started 6

Working Hard with Hardscape 12

A Natural Look 20

Being an "Outsider" 27

Problem Solving 28

Glossary 30

Index 31

Answer Key 32

Landscape Architects

Today, more and more families want to create living spaces outside. But it is not a matter of just bringing indoor things outdoors. They still want plants, flowers, **shrubs**, and trees.

This can be a big job. People might not know how to create these spaces themselves. What types of plants would be best? Do certain flowers attract butterflies? Can there be a stone fire pit for roasting marshmallows? Is there enough space for a path of rocks? There can be a lot to think about!

So, people call **landscape architects** to help. Landscape architects are different than other architects. Architects design buildings. Landscape architects plan for natural areas. Need plans for a house? Call an architect. Want the backyard to be designed? That is a job for a landscape architect! They have been trained to design beautiful outdoor spaces.

A landscape architect plans an outdoor living space that combines nature with other items.

Getting Started

Once landscape architects are hired, they need to ask their **clients** about their wants and needs. Some clients may be vegetable garden gurus. They want to grow their own meals. Others may be rose garden experts. They want the best red roses in town. Still others may be barbecue masters. They need a shady spot to grill. All of them may want to walk through their yards without getting dirty feet. Landscape architects ask a lot of questions. They listen carefully. It is their job to make these outdoor dreams come true.

To do so, landscape architects need two main types of supplies. They need **softscape** and **hardscape**. Natural things are softscape. These include the plants, flowers, shrubs, and trees that will be used. Things, such as paths, rocks, walls, and stone fire pits, which are added to nature, are hardscape. Landscape architects use these elements to create perfect outdoor spaces.

All that this outdoor area is missing is food and a willing cook!

These herbs and vegetables are almost ready to harvest.

LET'S EXPLORE MATH

Perimeter is the distance around a shape or figure. Imagine that a landscape architect draws a plan for a family's square vegetable garden. A rabbit fence will surround the garden. Why does the landscape architect need to know the perimeter?

After landscape architects learn about what their clients want, they ask themselves questions. How much space is needed? What are the best materials to use? Can a client's dream fit in the space?

For help, they may call a **surveyor**. Surveyors measure land. Then, they conduct **surveys**. Most surveys are conducted when land is bought or sold. Surveys are the process of taking measurements of a property. To take a survey, a yard surveyor places tiny pins at the four corners of a yard. Then, he or she measures the distance between the pins. The distances are used to calculate the amount of land that is owned.

Other landscape architects conduct their own surveys. They may use websites to help them. These can give **aerial** photos of yards. Landscape architects can then print them. The photos can help them measure the yards.

A surveyor takes measurements.

aerial view of a neighborhood

LET'S EXPLORE MATH

Imagine that a backyard is in the shape of a rectangle. The yard survey shows that two sides are 18 feet long. The other two sides are 16 feet long. A fence will surround the backyard. What is the perimeter of this backyard? Find two ways to prove your reasoning.

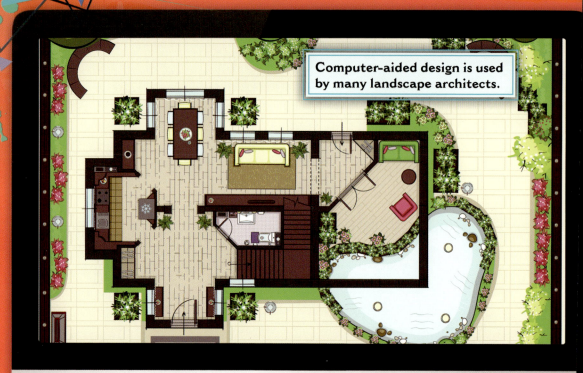

Computer-aided design is used by many landscape architects.

three-dimensional plan generated by computer software

When landscape architects are ready, they can make plans a few different ways. Computer programs may be used to draw ideas. Some of these programs even have three-dimensional views. Or, plans may be drawn by hand. If this is the case, draft paper and pencils are used.

Plans may even be drawn in the backyard with spray paint! Landscape architects use special marking paint to outline spaces where things will go. This helps clients easily see how space will be used. They can imagine what the finished space will look like. This is a good way to help people know early on if they want to change their minds.

Whether done on computer or by hand, plans have to be accurate. This is the only way to know where things will go and whether they will all fit. Details are added to make plans even more precise. Color may be used to make the plans clearer.

Hand-drawn plans can be precise and colorful.

Working Hard with Hardscape

The plans are finally done. The clients love the ideas. Now, it is time for landscape architects to bring those ideas to life. Projects can all be very different, so they have their work cut out for them.

Fencing the Yard

Fences are popular projects. Families with pets often want fences around their yards. This keeps their pets from running off. If there is a pool on the property, a fence might be needed to keep people safe. Sometimes, a fence is just there to show where a property ends.

There are many types of fences to choose from. Some are made from some very wild materials! But, most people choose something more ordinary. Some fences are made of metal, like **wrought iron**. There are plastic fences, too. Another popular type of fencing is treated wood. It looks natural and is **cost-effective**. Families can get a lot for their money. The treatment on the wood protects the fence from decay, weather, and bugs.

fence made from old surfboards

Wrought iron fences can have intricate patterns.

LET'S EXPLORE MATH

A landscape architect is installing a treated wood fence around a property. From the yard survey, she knows the property's land is in the shape of a rectangle. She also knows that the perimeter is 70 meters. The yard width is labeled as 25 meters on the survey. But, the yard's length got cut off! What is the length of the backyard?

Perimeter: 70 m

25 m   25 m

Planning the Perfect Patio

Many outdoor living spaces have patios that can be used as living and dining areas. Patios require plans that use hardscape.

It is very hard to move a patio once it is installed. It is often **cemented** into place! The stones and rocks can weigh a lot, too. So, it is important that measurements are correct the first time.

Precisely laid brick hardscape will form this patio.

Landscape architects need to know about furniture that might go onto patios. Many clients want to be able to eat outside. So, architects have to make the size of the hardscape bigger than the size of a table. This is so people have enough room to walk and to pull chairs away from the table. Chairs need to stay on the hardscape. No one wants to scoot onto soggy grass!

LET'S EXPLORE MATH

Find the perimeter of each rectangular tabletop.

Table	Length	Width	Perimeter
1	4 ft.	4 ft.	
2	6 ft.	3 ft.	
3	8 ft.	2 ft.	

This table and chair set was designed to look like mushrooms growing out of the grass.

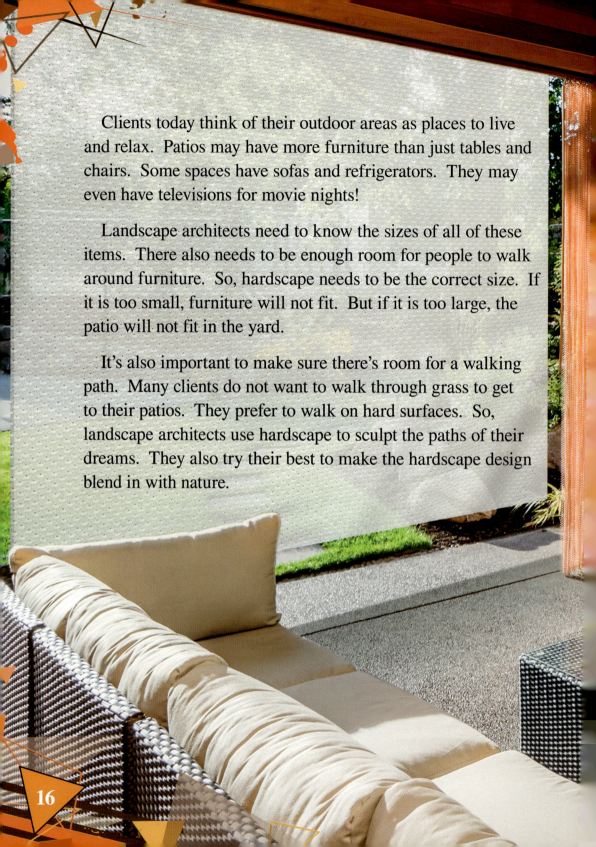

Clients today think of their outdoor areas as places to live and relax. Patios may have more furniture than just tables and chairs. Some spaces have sofas and refrigerators. They may even have televisions for movie nights!

Landscape architects need to know the sizes of all of these items. There also needs to be enough room for people to walk around furniture. So, hardscape needs to be the correct size. If it is too small, furniture will not fit. But if it is too large, the patio will not fit in the yard.

It's also important to make sure there's room for a walking path. Many clients do not want to walk through grass to get to their patios. They prefer to walk on hard surfaces. So, landscape architects use hardscape to sculpt the paths of their dreams. They also try their best to make the hardscape design blend in with nature.

LET'S EXPLORE MATH

A landscape architect is installing a rectangular path in a backyard. The family knows the length of the path. Now they need to decide the width. They want to choose a width based on the resulting perimeter.

1. Complete the table so the family can decide.

Length	Width	Perimeter
9 m	2 m	_____ m
9 m	3 m	_____ m
9 m	4 m	_____ m
9 m	5 m	_____ m

2. What do you notice about the perimeters? Why do you think this happened?

Setting Up for S'mores

Oozy chocolate, sweet graham crackers, and melted marshmallows combine for the perfect outdoor treat—s'mores! Or, perhaps you prefer crunchy marshmallows? Either way, they need to be roasted. This is just one reason many clients ask for fire pits in their yards.

For some pits, gas lines are put underground. Fire appears with the flip of a switch. For others, wood is used. These take a little longer to light. Either way, fire pits are made from hardscape. Often, there is hardscape around a fire pit, too. This way, clients can sit around the fire. They can have their chairs on a stable surface.

Safety is key when building fire pits. They cannot be under trees or roofs. No one wants a house to catch fire. So, landscape architects look for safe spaces. A space needs to be far away from trees or other structures. Knowing the perimeter of a fire pit can help people make these plans.

A Natural Look

   Outdoor spaces can be awesome! There can be patios, paths, furniture, and fire pits. Is anything missing? Nature is needed! An outdoor space might look bare with only hardscape. So, landscape architects add plants. This makes the yard come to life. They may add flowers, trees, and shrubbery, too.

These bushes conceal an air conditioner.

Planting with a Plan

Plants can be used to define a clear perimeter around a space. Landscape architects may choose to plant flowers right next to a fence. This way, they surround the yard. Sometimes trees are planted in the middle of a large grassy area. Flowers can surround a tree to make the space pop with color.

At times, people want to hide things in their yard. For example, an air conditioner may look big and out of place. Garbage cans might not look very pretty. Plants are the perfect camouflage. Tall plants can easily hide these eyesores.

Plants may also be arranged in flower beds. Landscape architects have a few ideas in mind when designing these. First, they may choose to plant flowers in groups. This means that one type of flower is not planted by itself. Instead, many are planted together. This results in a bigger splash of color. Extra border plants can also be planted surrounding a flower bed. This makes it look fuller. Or, flowers might be planted in a bed with shrubs to accent the space.

Next, landscape architects often choose three main colors of flowers. More than three colors might look messy. So instead, they vary the shades.

Finally, they plant flowers by height. Tall plants go in the back. Shorter plants go in the middle or up front. This way, they can be seen. Even smaller plants can border the perimeter of a flower bed.

A shrub stands behind flowers to fill this space.

Orange, yellow, and purple brighten this yard.

Tall flowers add dimension to this flower bed.

A lot of thinking goes into choosing plants. Not every plant will grow well in every space. Some plants need a lot of shade. For these areas, landscape architects might use black bat flowers. Or, they might choose to use yellow rattlesnake plants to make a snake-like border. Both of these plants do well in shade.

Others plants spring up in the sunshine. The obvious choice for a sun-loving plant is a cactus. But an exotic bird of paradise plant would do well there, too. Perhaps a golden egg plant can be placed in full sun with the bird of paradise!

Just like sun and shade, soil can also affect plants. In some places, there is a lot of rocky soil. The **fragrant** lavender plant grows well in those places. Other places have sandy soil. Crape myrtle trees, with their bright pink, red, or purple flowers, would be a good choice in those yards.

A plant's survival also depends on **climate**. For example, most palm trees grow best in warm climates. But, some can thrive in freezing temperatures. Landscape architects know this information. They help people pick the best plants for their yards.

flowers of a crape myrtle tree

bird of paradise

Being an "Outsider"

Do you think you have what it takes to be a true "outsider"? Maybe becoming a landscape architect is for you! To start, you should love the outdoors. Most landscape architects go to college to study math, art, and design. You also have to learn about plants and environments. When you have learned enough, you earn a **license** to do the job.

But, you don't have to wait to make the outdoors special. Take time to notice the way parks, yards, and gardens are planned. Measure the perimeter of an outdoor space. Plant a small vegetable or flower garden. Not enough room? It only takes one plant in a pot by a window to get you started!

Landscape architects want to make outdoor dreams come true. So, the next time you see a beautiful yard, thank a landscape architect. And think about what you can do to make the outdoors even better.

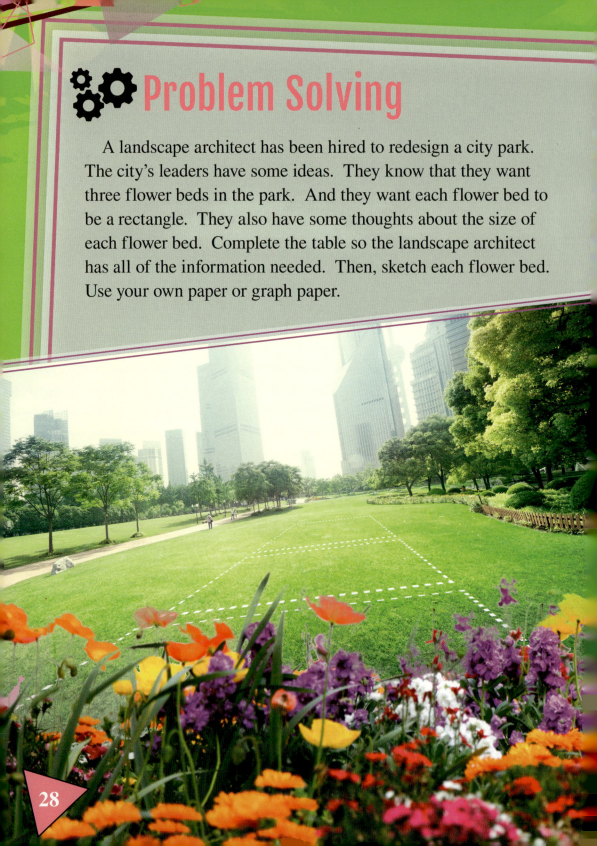

Problem Solving

A landscape architect has been hired to redesign a city park. The city's leaders have some ideas. They know that they want three flower beds in the park. And they want each flower bed to be a rectangle. They also have some thoughts about the size of each flower bed. Complete the table so the landscape architect has all of the information needed. Then, sketch each flower bed. Use your own paper or graph paper.

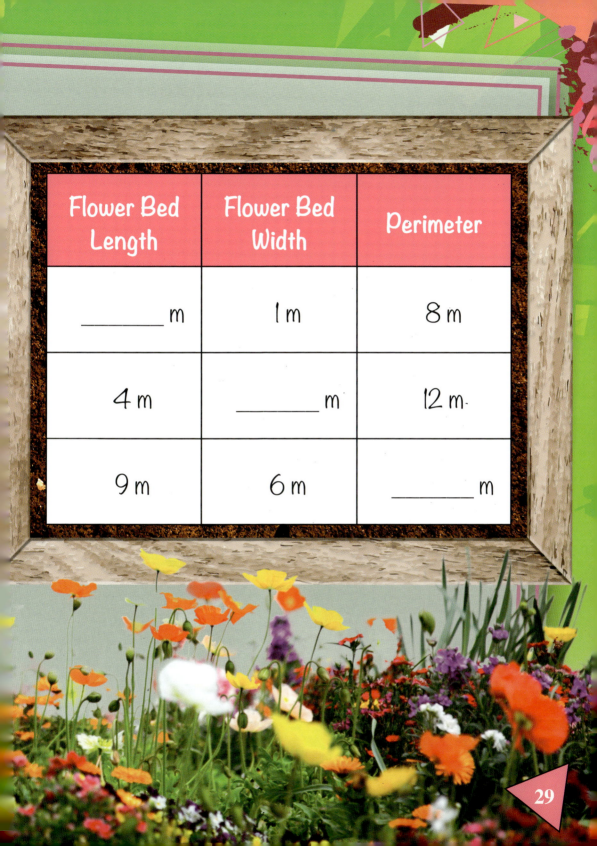

Flower Bed Length	Flower Bed Width	Perimeter
_____ m	1 m	8 m
4 m	_____ m	12 m
9 m	6 m	_____ m

Glossary

aerial—seen from above

cemented—joined together with concrete

clients—people who pay someone or a company for services

climate—the usual weather a place gets

cost-effective—producing good results without being too expensive

fragrant—having a pleasant smell

hardscape—the man-made fixtures of a planned outdoor area

landscape architects—people who design yards with hardscapes and plants

license—an official document that gives someone permission to do something

perimeter—the distance around the outside of a shape

shrubs—plants that have stems of wood and are smaller than trees

softscape—the natural elements of a planned outdoor area

surveyor—a person who measures and inspects areas of land

surveys—the act of measuring the dimensions of areas of land

wrought iron—a kind of iron that is used for decorative fencing

Index

bird of paradise, 24

black bat flowers, 24

cactus, 24–25

crape myrtle, 24

fire pit, 4, 6, 18–20

golden egg plant, 24

hardscape, 6, 12, 14–16, 19–20

lavender, 24–25

length, 13, 15, 17, 29

palm trees, 24–25

path, 4, 6, 16–17, 20

patio, 14–16, 20

rattlesnake plants, 24

shrubs, 4, 6, 23

softscape, 6

width, 13, 15, 17, 29, 32

wrought iron, 12–13

Answer Key

Let's Explore Math

page 7:
Perimeter helps the landscape architect know how many meters of fencing will be needed.

page 9:
68 ft.; Answers will vary but may include: 18 + 18 + 16 + 16, or (2 × 18) + (2 × 16).

page 13:
10 m

page 15:
Table 1: 16 ft.

Table 2: 18 ft.

Table 3: 20 ft.

page 17:
1.

Perimeter
22 m
24 m
26 m
28 m

2. The perimeters increase by 2 m because the width increases by 1 m each time, and there are two widths in a rectangle.

Problem Solving

Flower Bed Length: 3 m

Flower Bed Width: 2 m

Perimeter: 30 m

Sketches will vary but should show a 3 m by 1 m rectangle, a 4 m by 2 m rectangle, and a 9 m by 6 m rectangle.